Susanna Wesley

A Remarkable Woman and Mother

Sincerely,

George Rice

Susanna Wesley

A Remarkable Woman and Mother

by
George W. Rice

Beacon Hill Press of Kansas City
Kansas City, Missouri

Scripture quotation marked NKJV is taken from the *New King
James Version,* copyright ⓒ 1979, 1980, 1982, Thomas Nel-
son, Inc., Publishers. Used by permission.

10   9   8   7   6   5   4   3   2

Contents

Foreword

At a time when the role of motherhood is being questioned and sometimes downplayed, this little monograph has special pertinence.

Susanna Wesley was indeed "a remarkable woman and mother," one of the most remarkable in history. She found happiness and wholeness in losing herself for love of God and the significant others in her life—this despite marital, economic, and domestic problems that would have destroyed a lesser person.

These pages will introduce you to one who stands tall as a "woman for all seasons." Dr. Rice here captures and faithfully sketches the circumstances of her difficult existence, which never daunted her spirit.

Without benefit of formal education, Susanna became a philosopher-theologian in her own right and an effective schoolmarm and instructor of her ever-increasing brood. She was a spiritual leader and guide, not only for her own family but also for the Epworth parish during her parson-husband's frequent and often extended absences. She was fiercely loyal to her wifely vows but never hesitated to stand on her own two feet. To get the whole picture, you must read this story for yourself.

I am happy to recommend this little volume. It is an especially appropriate book for those who seek guidance and inspiration for their role as Christian women and mothers in these confused days.

—Dr. William M. Greathouse

Acknowledgments

Unless otherwise stated, quotations in this book are taken from the following two sources:

The Works of John Wesley, Third Edition, 14 vols., complete and unabridged. Reprinted 1978 by Beacon Hill Press of Kansas City, Kansas City, Mo., from the 1872 edition issued by Wesleyan Methodist Book Room, London.

The Journal of Charles Wesley, 2 vols. Reprinted 1980 by Beacon Hill Press of Kansas City, Kansas City, Mo., from the 1849 edition published by John Mason of London.

1

Susanna's Climate, Soil, and Roots

The birth year of Susanna Annesley, 1669, was not a good time to enter an English world of trouble and turmoil. The famous universities at Oxford and Cambridge were available for the rich and privileged elite, but common people had little or no opportunity to overcome their illiteracy. In this early dawn of the industrial revolution, children who would today have been enrolled in elementary schools were working long hours in sweatshops for a pittance to help support their poverty-stricken families. Malnutrition and disease were widespread. The social evils of lawlessness, violence, and drunkenness were commonplace. Along with flagrant crime there were extremes of punishment, so that a poor man could be hung for stealing a loaf of bread. Prison conditions were atrocious. Women had few rights and even fewer privileges.

A century of arrogant and extravagant rule

under misguided monarchs had caused many Englishmen to seek freedom in the new colonies in America. The turmoil climaxed finally in a civil war, followed by a brief experiment under kingless Puritan rule, which ended less than a decade before Susanna's birth in London. The city itself was in a confused period of reconstruction following London's Great Fire.

The year of Susanna's birth was also one of England's worst times with regard to organized religion. The Church of England served as the state religion. Among local curates were some faithful shepherds, but most were self-seeking and lifeless. Too many just "drew their breath and their salary," with little spiritual concern for their parishes or the deep needs of the people they were supposed to serve. They merely carried out their rituals of baptizing babies, marrying couples, and burying the dead. True, heartfelt religion was at a deplorably low ebb. Spiritual lethargy was the spirit of the times.

For two generations Nonconformist preachers had desperately tried to reform their church. But they were often driven out and as a result formed Dissenter churches. Dr. Samuel Annesley, Susanna's father, became a leader of this group, which rejected the autocracy and formalism of the established church. We know little about him, but he certainly shared the worthy goals of the best of the dissenting Puritans. These, as someone later described, were "to know God, to serve Him, and to enjoy Him." We know little about Susanna's mother, except that she was the daughter of a well-known London lawyer. She must have had an education far beyond the norm for girls of her time, if we are to judge by the training she gave her daughter Susanna.

Susanna was born the 25th child in the family of Dr. Samuel Annesley. As the baby of the home and her father's favorite child, Susanna might easily have grown to become an over-indulged, self-centered, and spoiled young lady. Instead she cultivated a genuine, natural piety. Early in life she felt God's call to a holy life and purposed never to spend more time in mere recreation in any day than she spent in private devotions.

We know nothing of the process of her education. This was an age long before the era of public schools, in a time when the only training thought necessary for girls was preparation to care for a home and to bear children. But in this climate Susanna Annesley was favored to receive an education far beyond that available to most boys of her day. She certainly learned to read, both well and widely, and made serious reading a lifetime habit. Her training must have included a clear understanding of theology, an interest she pursued avidly throughout her life. She later wrote a scholarly commentary on the Apostles' Creed. She was later able to read and evaluate, and to discuss with her son John, the theological merits of various scholars.

Susanna learned early in life to think for herself. While still in her teens, she made the decision to return to the established church. This must have taken a large degree of loving maturity, since her father was a leading Dissenter preacher.

2

Susanna's Early Marriage Years

Dr. Annesley, a dynamic person as well as an out-standing churchman, gathered about him a circle of friends and students, especially young preachers. They discussed and debated the issues of their day, especially those relating to the Dissenter position. One person in this group was a young Oxford student named Samuel Wesley, whose father and grandfather had been Nonconformist preachers. After examining both sides of this thorny question, Samuel chose to pursue ordination within the ranks of the established Church of England. Since Susanna had made a similar decision, he thus had an advantage in winning her affection.

Susanna was attractive beyond her pious spirit and disciplined mind. Centuries before modern beauty pageants, at least two of her older sisters were already famous beauties. Dr. Adam Clarke later referred to an accepted authority, who knew all the sisters well; he declared, "Beautiful as Miss (Judith) Annesley appears, she was far from being as beautiful as Mrs. Wesley." Young Samuel

Wesley was fortunate indeed to win the love, and the hand in marriage, of this attractive dissenting Dissenter. After Samuel graduated from Oxford, they were married in 1689. He was 26 years of age, and Susanna was 20.

As might be expected, with two such strong-minded partners, their marriage, though warmly stable, had continual adjustment and communication problems. During her later years, writing to her son John, she confessed, "It is an unhappiness almost peculiar to our family that your father and I seldom think alike." This is the only record we have when she allowed herself what one writer calls "the luxury of complaining." Though Susanna had much to complain about, she would probably have considered her statement as simply "stating the facts of life." Their mutual love and commitment, however, were more important than were their frequent disagreements.

Samuel and Susanna Wesley were always able to work through their differences. They apparently never lost their initial affection and respect for each other. This was important, for they received only minimal support from their rural parish communities. For the first 7 years the couple lived in small "opportunity" parishes, where Susanna gave birth to their first seven children. (Only four of them survived.) In 1697 they were assigned to the difficult parish of Epworth, a village in Lincoln County, England. This charge would certainly have qualified for what later American Methodists might call a "hard-scrabble" assignment. Samuel stayed on at Epworth as rector for the next 38 years, until his death in 1735. The problems of this lengthy pastorate may have influenced John Wesley's later decision to establish short-term, itinerant assignments for his Methodist preachers.

Susanna was blessed with a naturally strong constitution. She bore 19 children, including two sets of twins. She was often ill in connection with her pregnancies, the complications of childbirth, and other sicknesses common to that day. She lived in hardship most of the years in which she raised their large family. Yet she was 73 years old when she died.

This mistress of the manse was also, like her Lord, well "acquainted with grief" (Isa. 53:3). She experienced the sorrow of losing 9 of their 19 precious children. Most of these were stillborn or died as infants, including two sets of twins. As any mother of several children can bear testimony today, the number of children who remain never compensates for the death of a single, treasured loved one. Susanna was forced to carry the burden of her grief and yet to maintain a happy home climate for her husband and the other children.

Money was always in short supply. Their minimal yearly stipend left them in the constant grip of grinding poverty. Their parishioners apparently felt little or no obligation to supplement this meager salary. Samuel often antagonized many people in his parish, so that in turn, they frequently destroyed the rector's gardens. A few of his enemies stabbed and poisoned his cows and thus destroyed the family's milk supply. Much of this resistance came from the savagery of the barbarous inhabitants of the fens, or marshland surrounding Epworth. Perhaps Samuel's strong opinions, and his tendency to become personally involved in local politics, accounted for some of this opposition.

This antagonism, on one occasion, cost Susanna the life of a newborn child. Soon after a local election, an angry group gathered in the yard of the manse and spent the night "drumming, shouting, and firing off pistols and guns," in expression of their hatred. Susanna was still confined to bed, and a nurse was caring for her baby. This nurse, kept awake all night by the uproar, unknowingly "overlaid the child" and smothered it. One can only imagine Susanna's shock and grief when her dead baby was unceremoniously dumped on her bed by the frightened servants.

Perhaps seeking to supplement his meager income, Rector Samuel once became involved with a parishioner in what became an unsuccessful business venture. This man had his rector condemned to debtors' prison for a whole year, according to the extreme custom of that English era. Apparently no consideration was given for the added pressures on Susanna and her struggling family. Since prisoners in that day were forced to provide their own food, Susanna showed her love for Samuel by sending him her wedding ring, to be sold for food. The rector showed his love for Susanna by refusing to accept it or to sell her cherished possession. Somehow everyone survived.

During this extremely difficult year, Samuel's superior, the archbishop of York, visited the Epworth parsonage and asked Susanna "if she ever really wanted for bread." She replied, "I will freely own to your Grace that, strictly speaking, I never did want bread, but then I had so much care to get it before it was eaten, and to pay for it after, as has often made it unpleasant to me. [Had she lived today, we can imagine her resistance to our widespread credit card usage.] I think to have bread on such terms is the next degree of wretchedness to having none at all." (To his credit, the next morning the archbishop made a generous donation to the struggling young family.) These deprivations, cheerfully accepted, perhaps helped to train her famous sons, John and Charles, for their later hardships and life of voluntary poverty.

The strong opinions, political and otherwise, held by both Samuel and Susanna finally led to a major crisis in their marriage. Samuel was politically a confirmed Tory, and she was a Jacobite. Their son John later described this most serious disagreement: "The year before King William died, my father observed my mother did not say Amen to the prayer for the King. She said she could not; for she did not believe the Prince of Orange was [the true] King. He [Samuel] vowed he would never cohabit with her till she did. He then took his horse, and rode away [ostensibly on church business to Oxford]; nor did she hear anything of him for twelve months." Susanna continued on in the vicarage, carrying on her vital task of raising his children.

The death of King William early the next year brought to the English throne a monarch (Queen Anne) to whom both Samuel and Susanna could conscientiously give allegiance. This occasioned their reconciliation, and the rector returned to Epworth. The Church and the world would have been infinitely poorer had their differences remained unsettled. The next child born following their reconciliation was a boy named John. Charles was born three years later.

Susanna demonstrated unusual ability in managing such a large family and doing all this in a small, crowded house, with none of today's laborsaving devices. She did have the intermittent help of various servants, especially after she gave birth to a child. For the most part, however, she utilized the abilities and talents of the older children to help in the care and training of their younger siblings. She was able to maintain a climate of industry and tranquillity under crowded conditions

3

Susanna's School

Susanna had one task that today's mothers are normally able to turn over to others. In the absence of any public schools, training in the three Rs had to be done at home if it was to be done at all. Beginning with their first son, named for his father, Samuel, she established a regular routine of school, with hours from nine to twelve o'clock each weekday morning, and during the afternoons from two until five.

Hers was an age when a girl's usual education was only to learn to cook and to sew and to keep house. Remembering her own favored and exceptional childhood, Susanna refused to settle for less for her own daughters. As she declared, "Putting children to learn sewing before they can read perfectly, is the very reason, why so few women can read fit to be heard, and never to be well understood."

Each child's fifth birthday became his day of enrollment in Susanna's school. Preparations were made the previous day for household duties and homework assignments for the older siblings. Then, giving her undivided attention, during those six hours Susanna taught each five-year-old child the alphabet (both lowercase and uppercase). At first she thought her daughters Molly and Nancy were a little dull, because they "were a day and a half before they knew them perfectly." Later on she was better able to recognize her children's individual differences of ability and aptitude, and wrote, "I have changed my opinion."

The next day, having learned the letters, each kindergarten-age child began to read, beginning with the first verse in the Book of Genesis. Her method was simple and effective: "He was taught to spell the first verse, then to read it over and over, till he could read it off-hand without any hesitation; so on to the second, etc., till he took ten verses for a lesson." Susanna had learned the value of repetition and accountability. The children were not permitted to leave "till perfect in their lesson . . . and before we left school, each child read what he had learned . . . that day."

Lacking age-graded children's books, she went on to use other adult books after her biblical beginning. She shared with her children the excitement of recognizing words they had learned, when they saw those same words elsewhere. "By this means," she later observed, they "learned very soon to read an English author well." She expected much of her children, and they responded positively. She later wrote, "It is almost incredible, what a child may be taught in a quarter of a year, by a vigorous application, if it have but a tolerable capacity, and good health." This helps to explain the prodigious lifetime reading and study habits of her three preacher sons.

Learning was not easy or automatic in the Wesley home, but Susanna had the faith and patience of a true teacher. On one occasion her husband in exasperation asked her, "Why do you sit there teaching that dull child that lesson over the twentieth time?" Susanna gave a classic answer: "Had I satisfied myself by mentioning the matter only nineteen times, I should have lost all my labour. You see it was the twentieth time that crowned the whole." In this way Susanna prepared her three sons for college. John was 10 years old when he went to the Charter House School in London, where his brother Samuel had studied.

Susanna maintained consistent discipline in her crude classroom. She describes some simple ground rules: "Rising out of their places, or going out of the room, was not permitted, unless for good cause; and running into the yard, garden, or street, without leave, was always esteemed a capital offence." Apparently the Wesley family had those occasional problems normal to children of every time and place.

Susanna Wesley lived well over two centuries before Drs. Benjamin Spock and James Dobson, but she demonstrated unusual child-rearing wisdom. Admittedly, the Epworth home and school was a sheltered, protected environment. It was not particularly threatened by outside influences, as most modern homes face. But the principles she developed and practiced may well be useful today.

At her son John's request, she later recorded the principles that she had faithfully followed in rearing all her children:

1. Devise a regular routine of living in all areas of their life.
2. Develop proper study habits early and consistently.
3. Teach proper table manners early in their life.
4. Never allow drinks or snacks between meals.
5. Teach them to have private devotions, morning and evening.
6. Maintain regular family devotions, showing proper respect.
7. Maintain respect for everyone else's person and property.

8. Enforce unfailing courtesy, even toward siblings.
9. Allow no habits to form that must later be broken.
10. Give the child nothing for which he cries.
11. Commend and reward special acts of obedience.
12. Respect the Sabbath, giving much adult time to children.
13. Maintain purity of language, avoiding slang and crudeness.
14. Recognize and accept differences in aptitude and ability.
15. Accept problems of interruption and distraction.
16. Assign regular and consistent family chores.
17. Keep proper priority of work and study.
18. Accept responsibility for the home teaching of children.
19. Conquer the will of children (without breaking the spirit).
20. Maintain consistent discipline.
    a. Encourage open confession and forgiveness of wrongs.
    b. Commend and reward all acts of obedience.

   c. Let no sinful act go unpunished, then
     never upbraid again.
   d. Accept intention rather than perfect
     performance.
   e. Maintain proper priorities.

Elaborating on this principle, Susanna declared in strong, almost impassioned words: "No indulgences [of self-will] can be trivial, no denial unprofitable. Heaven or hell depends on this alone. So that the parent who studies to subdue it in his child, works together with God in the renewing and saving a soul. The parent who indulges it does the devil's work, makes religion impracticable, salvation unattainable; and does all that in him lies to damn his child, soul and body for ever."

4

Susanna's Kitchen Evangelism

It should be noted that Susanna was not alone in her concern for the spiritual welfare of her children. Her son Charles recalled hearing his father say, "God has shown me I shall have all my nineteen children about me in heaven." This impression led Charles to express his own similar faith: "I have the same blessed hope for my eight."

One episode in Susanna's life reveals much about her courage and loving concern for her family's spiritual nurture. Samuel had gone to Oxford on one of his frequent church business trips, as a clerical delegate from his district. He appointed a certain unworthy curate to be in charge of the Epworth parish in his absence. This careless assistant was dull and dry as a public speaker, and he canceled the customary Sunday night service.

Susanna proceeded to make up the difference. She wrote to Samuel: "As I am a woman, so I am also mistress of a large family. . . . in your absence, I cannot but look upon every soul you leave under my care, as a talent committed to me under a trust,

26

by the great Lord of all the families, both of heaven and earth. ... [This] made me ... take a more than ordinary care of the souls of my children and servants."

Susanna began devoting Sunday evenings to the practice of "reading to and instructing my family." Soon a neighbor's family asked permission to join them. Before long revival had begun. That small Epworth parsonage kitchen was soon crowded with 30 or 40 neighbors and friends. At times the number increased to 200, inside and outside the house. Along with songs and Scripture reading, Susanna began to read to them her husband's "best and most awakening sermons."

The jealous interim curate wrote to Rector Samuel at Oxford, charging that Susanna was violating church rules by her "preaching," and that this reflected badly on Samuel for permitting such a "scandal." Her disturbed husband wrote immediately, "desiring" Susanna to stop this unorthodox practice. (By now her congregation was larger than the curate's Sunday morning congregation.)

Susanna answered Samuel in a classic letter: "I cannot conceive, why any should reflect upon you, because your wife endeavours to draw people to church, and to restrain them from profaning the Lord's day, by reading to them, and other persuasions. ... As to its looking particular, I grant it does. And so does almost any thing that is serious, or that may any way advance the glory of God, or the salvation of souls. .... For my part, I value no censure upon this account. I have long since *shook hands with the world*" (italics added).

She then went on to explain the origin of the predicament. Through reading a certain missionary book, she related, "It came into my mind, Though I am not a man, nor a Minister, yet if my heart were sincerely devoted to God, and I was inspired with a true zeal for his glory, I might do somewhat more than I do. I thought I might pray more for them, and might speak to those with whom I converse with more warmth of affection. I resolved to begin with my own children." She began by scheduling a separate time to "discourse with each child." John was assigned an hour on Thursday night. Years later he wrote to his mother, asking her to pray especially for him at the same hour she had formerly given for those conversations that had helped him so much in forming proper judgments.

News of this revival in the manse spread, and, as Susanna explained, "With those few neighbours that then came to me, I discoursed more freely and affectionately." One wonders if some of these neighbors had been among those who earlier had made life miserable for the parsonage family. At any rate, Susanna evangelized many of her neighbors and friends.

Samuel had suggested that Susanna might enlist a man to read his sermons, but she pointedly reminded him, "I do not think one man among them could read a sermon, without spelling a good part of it. Nor has any of our family a voice strong enough [as yet] to be heard by such a number of people." (Both John and Charles would later be clearly heard and understood, without any modern technological helps, by crowds that sometimes numbered as many as 20,000 people.)

Susanna honestly questioned the propriety of a woman "presenting the prayers of the people to God." But she went on to explain to her husband, "Last Sunday I would fain have dismissed them before prayers; but they begged so earnestly to stay, I durst not deny them."

Then Samuel, certainly under pressure from his small-minded interim curate, wrote her that he desired the meetings to be stopped. Susanna's answer must have jarred him: "If you do after all, think fit to dissolve this assembly, do not tell me that you *desire* it, for that will not satisfy my conscience; but send me your positive command in such full and express terms as may absolve me from all guilt and punishment, for neglecting this opportunity of doing good, when you and I shall appear before the great and awful tribunal of our Lord Jesus Christ." We can understand why Samuel wrote nothing more about the matter.

5

Susanna Influencing Her Children

Perhaps the most outstanding event connected with the Epworth parish was the infamous parsonage fire. (Some historians credit this to the work of an arsonist opposed to Rector Samuel.) The family was providentially awakened and fled to safety, all except six year old John, who was trapped in his upstairs bedroom. Assembled neighbors saw his face at the window and heard his cry for help. One man stood on another man's shoulders and pulled the child out of the window, just moments before the burning roof caved inward.

This experience had a profound effect on the boy, who later frequently pictured himself as "a brand plucked from the burning." Many years afterward, in describing a London watch-night service, John Wesley wrote: "About eleven o'clock it came into my mind, that this was the very day and hour in which, forty years ago, I was taken out of the flames. I stopped, and gave a short account of that wonderful providence. The voice of praise and thanksgiving went up on high, and great was our rejoicing before the Lord."

"Jackie's" unusual deliverance deepened his parent's desire to devote special effort in training him. He had been miraculously spared, they were assured, and God must have some special purpose and work for his future. They did not dream how useful his life would become, both in his own generation and in future centuries.

When the house was rebuilt, Susanna added a vital practice to her family's routine, which had far-reaching implications. As she described it: "Then was begun the custom of singing psalms at beginning and leaving school, morning and evening." This special emphasis on music certainly made a deep impression on the mind and heart of her youngest boy. Charles Wesley, growing up in this atmosphere of devotional music, was to become one of the most prolific hymn writers of the entire Church in all the Christian era.

Susanna's personal faith and devotion, and her quickened concern for others, were perhaps the outstanding qualities of her life and example. Her sons John and Charles later sought to make these same qualities the foundation of their Holy Club efforts at Oxford University. As she had reached out to her neighbors in Epworth, they now ministered to the unfortunate in jails and poverty areas near the university. It was their careful, systematic, religious practice, instilled in them by home training, that gave them the then-derisive name of Methodists. Susanna's courage and faith in dealing with Epworth's antagonisms would become a memory bulwark to them as they faced the animosity of mobs and the misguided clerical opposition to their mighty movement.

While at Oxford, John Wesley was struggling to find the key to living a holy life, both for himself and for his Holy Club. He wrote to his mother about this theological problem. In a letter dated June 18, 1725, Susanna gave him this practical answer, in words that still offer classic advice for younger and older people of every generation and circumstance: "Take this rule; Whatever weakens your reason, impairs the tenderness of your conscience, obscures your sense of God, or takes off your relish of spiritual things; in short, whatever increases the strength and authority of your body over your mind: that thing is sin to you, however innocent it may be in itself."

One modern historian has aptly summarized Susanna's profound influence upon Methodism: "She instilled in John a love for method and order, a deep appreciation of learning and books, studious and economical ideas, and a sincere reverence for God."

Susanna developed a zeal for outreach long before the modern missionary movement. Reading a book about the Danish missionaries at Tranquebar made a deep impression on this hard-working wife and mother. The experience proved to be far more than just a fleeting emotional stimulation. She never lost her missionary vision.

Years later her son John, who was struggling to find spiritual reality for himself, was invited to go to America as a missionary to the Indians in the colony of Georgia. Charles was asked to accompany him and to serve as secretary to James Oglethorpe, governor of the colony and a longtime friend of the Wesley family. Their father, Samuel, had recently died, and John felt a deep obligation to "be the staff of [his mother's] age, her chief support and comfort." He prayerfully decided to allow Susanna to decide his course of action. General Oglethorpe later described how Susanna cast her deciding vote for world missions. In his words, "This noble-minded woman declared, 'Had I twenty sons, I should rejoice that they were all so employed, though I should never see them more.'" Thus released to serve, John and Charles sailed to St. Simons Island in Georgia.

God used a severe storm during this trip to America to introduce the Wesley brothers to the faith of certain German Christians. Even the women and children of these Moravians demonstrated a surer faith in Christ during the raging storm than the two staid clerics had thought possible. This helped to bring them under deep conviction, and they became earnest seekers after spiritual reality and "the assurance of faith."

Susanna had poured into her children her appreciation and love for the Bible. She had helped them to learn to read from the Scriptures. She had taught them to "trust and obey" God's precepts as best they understood them. It is no accident that John Wesley's sermons were constantly built around quotation and application of God's Word. His Letters and daily Journal are Scripture-soaked. Any study of the "psalms and hymns and spiritual songs" (Col. 3:16) of her son Charles shows them to be rich with Scripture quotation or Bible-related illustration and application. Susanna had helped to establish their Bible study habits. It was indeed fortunate, for her generation and the future Church, that John and Charles Wesley never outgrew her pattern.

Susanna had modeled self-possession and organizational genius as she carried out her task as wife, mother, and parish assistant. John Wesley later expressed his admiration for "the calm serenity with which his mother transacted business, wrote letters, and conversed, surrounded by her thirteen children." He could wish later in his life that he might, under God, manage the Methodist movement with equal grace and effectiveness.

Another example of Methodism's genius and incentive for growth was John Wesley's concept of small group meetings. In these class meetings each person was carefully accountable to another member for his actions and religious experience. John Wesley had learned the value of this on countless Thursday nights, when his mother had shared his problems, as well as hers, and clarified his judgments. Why shouldn't this work on a larger scale? History proves that it did, far beyond his fondest hopes. As at Epworth, the exact method to be used grew out of realized practical needs.

This writer once heard a secular scholar, teaching in a major American university, declare: "If I wanted to make any group of people feel a part of their church, enjoy close fellowship, grow in their personal experience, and be accountable for their progress, I would set up a system like the class meeting idea John Wesley developed over 200 years ago. The midweek prayer and testimony service practiced by many churches is the closest modern application of this principle."

Susanna was never stingy with advice to her grown-up children, even when they didn't ask her opinion. On one occasion, John was incensed that Thomas Maxfield, a layman, had dared to preach the gospel. Susanna admonished him: "John, you know what my sentiments have been; you cannot suspect me favouring readily anything of this kind: but take care what you do with respect to that young man, for he is as surely called of God to preach as you are. Examine what have been the fruits of his preaching, and hear him also yourself." Susanna's son took her advice, and then said, "It is the Lord: let him do as seemeth to him good" (see 1 Sam. 3:18). Lay preaching, which across the years has been such a tremendous boon to the evangelical movement, was thus given a powerful impetus.

We have no record of Susanna's response to John Wesley's break with tradition, when he followed George Whitefield's example of field preaching to the spiritually neglected miners at Kingswood. John had been a very correct and proper presbyter of the Church of England. He declared that he had been "so tenacious of every point relating to decency and order, that I should have thought the saving of souls almost a sin if it had not been done in a church."

But now, as he tells us, "At four [o'clock] I submitted to be more vile, and proclaimed in the highways the glad tidings of salvation to about three thousand people." In the years ahead, he reached as many as 20,000 people in a single service by this "vile" method. Once he was denied access to the Epworth church, where his father had given a lifetime of dedicated service. He stood on his father's tombstone outside the church and declared God's good news. (This was his privilege, because the family owned the grave site.) We can assume that Susanna, remembering her "kitchen" church at Epworth, must have heartily supported this new approach. Her mind-set certainly included going to those who, for any reason, could not or would not come through the channels of the church. She had planted seeds that grew into John's conviction that "the world is my parish."

The Inward Witness Among the Wesleys

Susanna's children were grown and away from home when her husband died in 1735 in the 46th year of their marriage. A faithful pastor until his death, Samuel Wesley, too, had emphasized this "inner assurance of faith" that God offers to all His obedient, believing children. In his Journal, John recorded the old Epworth rector's last words, three years before Aldersgate: "The inward witness, my son . . . this is the proof, the strongest proof of Christianity." This conscious assurance of his father's acceptance with God, and the Savior's atoning forgiveness of sins, must have made a great impact on the future founder of Methodism.

Only eternity will reveal all the influences that brought John Wesley to his famous Aldersgate experience. May 24, 1738, has a permanent place in history along with Paul's Damascus road conversion and Augustine's transformation in the garden of a Roman villa. John testifies simply that: "In the evening I went very unwillingly to a society in Aldersgate Street, where one was reading Luther's preface to the Epistle to the Romans. About a quarter before nine, while he was describing the change which God works in the heart through faith in Christ, I felt my heart strangely warmed. I felt I did trust in Christ, Christ alone for salvation: And an assurance was given me, that he had taken away *my* sins, even *mine*, and saved *me* from the law of sin and death." It was, in the words of T. Crichton Mitchell, "The greatest day of the 18th century, and in some ways the greatest event in the history of the modern Church—the conversion of John Wesley!"

Earlier in this same week, Charles Wesley had been led into the same evangelical experience. It is interesting to note that God used writings by the founder of Protestantism to bring the assurance of faith to this hungering, thirsting preacher and hymn writer also. As Charles read Martin Luther's commentary on Galatians, the effect on him was dynamic. He describes its results: "From this time I endeavoured to ground as many of our friends as came in this fundamental truth, salvation by faith alone, not an idle, dead faith, but a faith which works by love, and is necessarily productive of all good works and all holiness."

Susanna Wesley had her own personal heart-warming encounter, soon after John's Aldersgate experience. Her sons Charles and John had been helped toward their "evangelical awakening" by light from Martin Luther's words about true faith. The occasion of Susanna's "witness of the Spirit" was during a regular Communion service. Seventy years old at the time, she testified that while her son-in-law Hall "was pronouncing those words . . . 'The blood of our Lord Jesus Christ, which was given for thee;' [they] struck through my heart, and I knew God for Christ's sake had forgiven *me* all *my* sins." In this decisive moment, the exciting Great Evangelical Revival had begun in her heart.

Susanna Wesley had been naturally critical, at first, of the heartwarming experience of her sons John and Charles. After all, she had trained them carefully and rigidly. They were already ordained ministers and had even served as missionaries to America. Why did they need anything else to confirm their faith? She herself had lived a whole life of deep devotion, rigid discipline, and exalted principles. Wasn't that enough witness to her "rightness" with God? But God knew her need and gave her the witness of the Spirit that she was truly a child of the King.

It is of interest to note the different circumstances under which this historic family responded to God's call to spiritual reality. John's heart was "strangely warmed" in a public service of worship. Charles experienced his evangelical awakening during a time of private study and devotion. Susanna came to realize her personal assurance while being served the elements of Communion. Perhaps we can conclude there is no one "right way" to seek and find God's similar blessing.

On one occasion, several persons who identified true religion only with inner "stillness" tried to infiltrate and influence Wesley's group. These misguided extremists had come to regard the sacraments as mere outward and unnecessary "crutches," matters of duty unworthy of true "inward" Christians. They dealt with his mother, "but all in vain," was John's record. "Bishop B. would as soon have given up the ordinances as she." He well remembered that it was during a Communion service that Susanna's heart had been consciously touched by God's Spirit. He had no fear that she would forsake these blessed "means of grace," which had been the occasion of her inward "assurance of faith."

Susanna lived with John for extended periods of time in her later years, at his Foundery residence in London, the headquarters of the Methodist movement. He frequently notes her traveling with him to a nearby assignment. What joy and pride she must have felt as she remembered the night when he had become "a brand plucked from the burning." The God who had so miraculously spared John Wesley had now made him into a firebrand who spread his heartwarming message across the length and breadth of the British Isles.

John Wesley had no children of his own, but he did candidly evaluate Susanna's dealings with his nieces and nephews. In his sermon "On the Education of Children," John later wrote, "In fourscore years I have not met with one woman that knew how to manage grandchildren. My own mother, who governed her children so well, could never govern one grandchild." Today's grandmothers may take comfort from this testimony and understand why, as someone recently observed, "God gives this biggest job in the world to rank amateurs."

6

Susanna's Homegoing

John Wesley once observed, "Our people die well," with the kind of trust that carries them victoriously through the last "valley of the shadow of death" (Ps. 23:4). Susanna's death on July 23, 1742, almost exactly 73½ years from her birth, certainly modeled his later testimony about those early Methodists. As John described the scene in his Journal: "I found my mother on the borders of eternity. But she had no doubt or fear; nor any desire but (as soon as God should call), 'to depart, and to be with Christ.' . . . I sat down on the bedside. She was in her last conflict; unable to speak, but I believe quite sensible. Her look was calm and serene, and her eyes fixed upward, while we commended her soul to God. [An hour later,] without any struggle, or sigh, or groan, the soul was set at liberty. We stood round the bed, and fulfilled her last request, uttered a little before she lost her speech: 'Children, as soon as I am released, sing a psalm of praise to God.'"

We are not told which praise song Susanna's

children sang. A hymn written later by her son Charles to commemorate George Whitefield may well have expressed their sentiments:

> *Servant of God, well done!*
> *Thy glorious warfare's past;*
> *The battle's fought, the race is won,*
> *And thou art crowned at last.*
>
> . . . .
>
> *Redeemed from earth and pain,*
> *O when shall we ascend,*
> *And all in Jesus' presence reign*
> *Through ages without end?*

With tearful eyes and unsteady voice, John Wesley preached his mother's funeral sermon. He chose as his text, "I saw a great white throne, and him that sat on it . . ." He described her funeral as "one of the most solemn assemblies I ever saw, or expect to see on this side eternity." She was buried in Bunhill Fields cemetery in City Road, London. Her grave site, not far from where John would be buried 49 years later, ranks today with Westminster Cathedral as one of London's primary tourist attractions for evangelicals from around the world.

It was appropriate that on the plain stone at the head of Susanna's grave should be the simple inscription: "Here lies the body of Mrs. Susanna Wesley, the youngest and last surviving daughter of Dr. Samuel Annesley." On this same marker are verses written by her son Charles, beautifully picturing her earthly tragedies and her heavenly triumph:

> *In sure and steadfast hope to rise,*
> *And claim her mansion in the skies,*
> *A Christian here her flesh laid down,*
> *The cross exchanging for a crown.*
>
> *True daughter of affliction, she,*
> *Inured to pain and misery,*
> *Mourn'd a long night of griefs and fears,*
> *A legal night of seventy years.*

Susanna Annesley Wesley, faithful Christian, wife, and mother, died "in sure and steadfast hope" of her eternal reward. She had been devoted as a teenager, giving God first place in all areas of her life. She had maintained her love for a man who was not always easy to live with. She had followed God as a pastor's wife, faithfully fulfilling her duties, and giving far beyond the demands of mere duty. As a mother she had excelled, modeling, teaching, and loving her children. As a Christian, she faithfully served a Savior who had made himself real to her during a Communion service. We can almost hear His words of glad welcome at heaven's gate: "Well done, good and faithful servant; you have been faithful over a few things, I will make you ruler over many things. Enter into the joy of your Lord" (Matt. 25:23, NKJV).

7

The Fruit of Susanna's Labors

Susanna Wesley lived only four years after her son's Aldersgate experience. This was long enough for her to witness the beginnings of the Great Evangelical Revival, which in John's lifetime literally transformed England. Paul described the role of the ancient Mosaic law as "our schoolmaster to bring us unto Christ" (Gal. 3:24). God used this devoted mother to achieve the same goal in John's life.

Particularly in his early years of revivalism, John Wesley and his followers endured massive persecution and even physical abuse. These attacks were usually inspired by parsons selfishly "guarding their turf" against open-air preaching that disregarded parish boundaries. Often this opposition took the less violent form of literary attacks by letters and pamphlets. As a result, the Wesleyan movement gained nationwide publicity and sympathy from the general public. Methodism was on the move.

John and Charles Wesley, under God, raised up a devoted and growing army of preachers and people. John was certainly, as one historian observed, "a natural leader of men who excited their lively respect, obedience, and affection." Susanna's son lived long enough to place upon the movement his unmistakable stamp of spiritual charisma and organizational genius.

Wesley's success as preacher and leader cannot be separated from the gospel message he and his followers proclaimed. He constantly declared the good news of God's invitation to *a more abundant life*. "He taught men that they could accept God's grace by faith, could enjoy it, and possess it to the full." The church of Wesley's generation was hungry for spiritual reality and Spirit fullness.

Susanna's son Charles filled a vital role in earlier and later Methodism. A great revivalist and field preacher in his own right, Charles' major contribution was his poetry and music. Charles Wesley wrote more than 8,000 hymns and gospel songs. Some of his biographers declare that his musical contribution was as important to Methodism as John's theology. No doubt the hymns written by Susanna's 18th child were the embodiment of the brothers' doctrinal emphases.

Dozens of Wesley hymns are still included in the favorite music of most denominations today. Christians of every theological and denominational persuasion have been blessed as they join hearts and voices in exalting God and expressing their deepest devotional desires.

Reading the list of the hymns of Charles Wesley can be a devotional commentary for any Christian who appreciates Bible truth.

The following are some of his most famous:

"A Charge to Keep I Have"
"Arise, My Soul, Arise"
"I Do Believe"
"Jesus, Thine All-victorious Love"
"Love Divine, All Loves Excelling"
"O for a Heart to Praise My God"
"Rejoice, the Lord Is King"

Christians of every denomination have been lifted up in celebrating special holy seasons as they sing "Come, Thou Long-expected Jesus," "Hark! the Herald Angels Sing," and "Christ, the Lord, Is Risen Today."

Charles wrote one of his most famous hymns that aptly describes his spiritual Aldersgate. Out of his newfound joy and peace, he penned the words:

And can it be that I should gain
  An int'rest in the Saviour's blood!
Died He for me, who caused His pain?
  For me, who Him to death pursued?
Amazing love! How can it be
That Thou, my God, shouldst die for me?

Susanna's own spiritual pilgrimage, as well as that of her youngest son, is expressed in another verse of the hymn.

Long my imprisoned spirit lay,
  Fast bound in sin and nature's night.
Thine eyes diffused a quick'ning ray.
  I woke; the dungeon flamed with light.
My chains fell off; my heart was free.
I rose, went forth, and followed Thee.

What an investment Susanna had made in her baby boy, taught from infancy to sing psalms, in the prayerful spirit he later expressed in poetic music:

O for a heart to praise my God,
  A heart from sin set free,
A heart that always feels Thy blood
  So freely shed for me!

Devoted Susanna, nursing her infant son, certainly prayed in spirit for what that boy later expressed in exalted meter.

A heart resigned, submissive, meek,
  My great Redeemer's throne,
Where only Christ is heard to speak,
  Where Jesus reigns alone.

John Wesley shared his brother's devotion. He never allowed the importance of his work to sap his personal spiritual vitality, amid all the pressures as leader of an increasingly thriving church. He rose early every morning, reminiscent of Susanna's training at Epworth, and devoted many hours daily to prayer and devotional reading.

Perhaps he summarized this best in his Journal in December of 1744: (23) "I found such light and strength as I never remember to have had before." (25) "About eight, being with two or three that believed in Jesus, I felt such an awe and tender sense of the presence of God as greatly confirmed me therein: So that God was before me all the day long. I sought and found him in every place; and could truly say, when I lay down at night, 'Now I have *lived* a day.'"

John Wesley learned and constantly practiced the art of praying and reading as he rode on horseback and by carriage. His saddlebags were always stuffed with books, for himself and for his preachers. Someone has said, "In no other life was the balance between the culture of the soul and the service of people so exquisitely maintained."

If the quip is true that "behind every great man stands a great woman," then Susanna's part in the rise and spread of the Methodist movement cannot be overexaggerated. She stood squarely behind her two great sons.

Six years after Aldersgate, the Methodist Conference was born. The purpose of this infant organization was to discuss: "what to teach, how to teach, and what to do." By the time of John Wesley's death, Methodism, under several conferences, had spread all over the United Kingdom and had gathered at least 75,000 "numbers in the Society," in 115 circuits. Chapels flourished everywhere Methodism reached. Schools were organized, first for miners' children, then for the education of preachers' sons. Many of today's leading Bible schools, colleges, and seminaries, on several continents, can trace their origin to John Wesley and the Evangelical Awakening.

John Wesley never abandoned his simple life-style. He refused to profit personally from his great evangelical enterprise. As his income increased from offerings and writings, he gave to the cause and to the poor. When he died, he left behind, as someone has described: "A well-worn saddle, six shillings, a silver spoon, and the Methodist church."

John, like his mother, Susanna, never separated from the established church, though continual efforts were made by the Episcopal clergy to drive him forth. Six years before his death, however, he signed the Deed of Declaration, which made the annual Conference of Methodism the heir and preserver of his efforts. Perhaps the most important boon to American Methodism came when in 1784 Wesley ordained and sent four elders to the colonies and commissioned Thomas Coke as superintendent for America. This led to the famous "Christmas Conference" at Baltimore. There Francis Asbury was elected and consecrated superintendent, and the Methodist Episcopal church was organized in America.

Today, in addition to the parent United Methodist church, many other thriving evangelical groups are direct offshoots of the Evangelical Revival. One modern historian lists 35 present-day denominations that have their theological rootage in the Wesleyan movement. The challenge to every child of Methodism, whatever the denomination, is to seek and find and maintain the personal heartwarming reality John Wesley experienced at Aldersgate and his mother, Susanna, realized in a historic Communion service.

All Wesleyan believers owe a tremendous spiritual debt to John and Charles Wesley. Only God knows how much of this debt is owed to Susanna Annesley Wesley, a truly remarkable woman and mother.